Usborne

Little Children's
Nature
Activity
Book

Rebecca Gilpin

Designed and illustrated by

Non Figg, Erica Sirotich, Laurent Kling,

Camilla Garofano, Stephanie Fizer Coleman, Sr. Sánchez,

Pau Morgan, Peter Allen and Patrick Girouard

Edited by Fiona Watt

You'll find the answers
to the puzzles on
pages 61-64.

What is nature?

Where will you find it?

It's up in the air...

How many ducks are flying by?

....

...and all around you.

Which two ladybirds are the same?

It's by the sea...

Colour the shells.

...and under the ground.

Can you spot a smiling worm?

Read the words around each white circle and press on the matching nature stickers from the sticker pages.

crashing waves

a bird singing

plants growing

tall, tall trees

fluffy clouds

fish swimming

a hungry rabbit

rain falling

a dazzling sunrise

busy ants

Signs and clues

Footprints, nests, trails and nibbled bits of food all show where animals have been.

Can you work out which animal left each footprint? Read the descriptions, then write the correct letter next to each print.

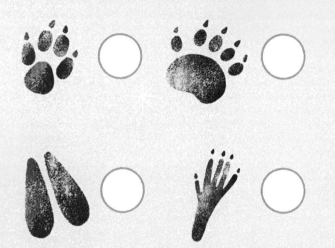

A. Badger –
five toes
with claws

B. Fox –
four toes
with claws

C. Deer –
a hoof in
two halves

D. Rat –
long and thin
with five toes

This duck has left some prints, but which ones?
Read the clues to discover the answer.

....

* They're not the biggest.
* They're not in pairs.
* They have webs of skin between the toes.

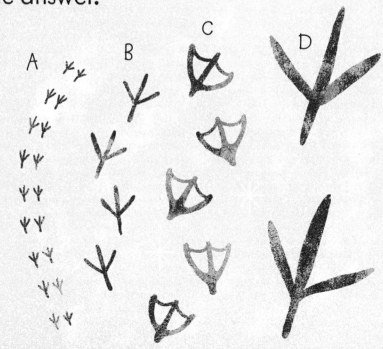

A   B   C   D

Follow the red lines to find out which harvest mouse made the round nest.

....

Draw along this snail's trail of slime as quickly as you can, without touching the sides.

A squirrel has nibbled one of the nuts lying among these leaves. Can you spot the nibbled nut?

Plants and trees

Many plants grow from seeds. When a seed splits, roots and shoots start to grow. Leaves then grow from the shoots. Can you put these pictures in order, from 1 to 5?

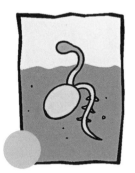 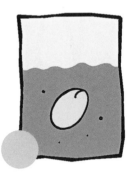 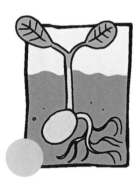  

When a shoot breaks out of the soil, it's called a seedling. Which of these seedlings is tallest?

How many matching pairs of plants are there below? ....

6

Trees are tall plants with woody trunks and branches.
They are home to birds, animals and insects.

Find the pictures below in the picture above, then colour them in.

a bird
cleaning its
feathers

toadstools
growing on a
tree trunk

a squirrel
leaping along
a branch

a woodpecker
feeding its
babies

patches of
moss on a
tree stump

Different kinds of animals

There are millions of kinds of animals. They all fit into different groups. Find the animal stickers on the sticker pages and put them in the right groups.

Birds have feathers, wings and beaks. They lay eggs.

goose

gull

sparrow

owl

Insects are tiny. They have six legs and two feelers on their heads.

moth

fly

ant

butterfly

bee

Amphibians have soft, damp skin. They can live on land and in water.

toad

frog

newt

Mammals give birth to their babies and feed them their milk.

cow

squirrel

seal

rabbit

Reptiles have dry, scaly skin. Most of them lay eggs.

snake

turtle

lizard

Fish are covered with scales and live in water.

mackerel

salmon

trout

stickleback

Insects

There are more insects on Earth than any other kind of creature. They each have six legs and most of them have wings. Look at the pictures below – which one is not an insect?

The insects below are good at hiding. Where could each one hide? Write the correct letter on each hiding place.

A

B

C

D

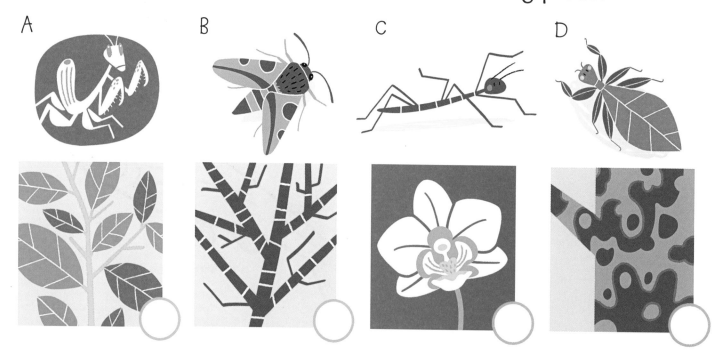

Can you label the parts of this fly? Read the words in the list, then write the correct number in each circle.

1. leg
2. thorax (middle)
3. antenna (feeler)
4. abdomen (end)
5. head
6. wing
7. eye

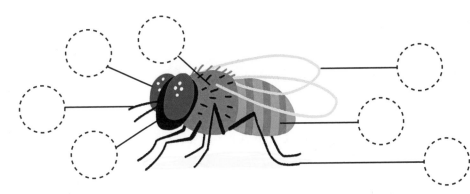

Butterflies are insects with four wings. Colour the butterflies in the picture below to match these two.

small tortoiseshell

common blue

Bird life

Most birds build nests, then lay eggs in them.
This pigeon is building a nest and has one last twig to add.
Which way does it need to fly to get back to the nest?

There's a different number of eggs in each of these swans' nests.
Which nest has most eggs?

A

.... eggs

B

.... eggs

C

.... eggs

Nest .... has most eggs.

Baby birds hatch out of their eggs and are fed by their parents.
Which route should the blackbirds take to feed their chicks?

Route ....

Route ....

Can you spot five differences between the two pictures below?
Draw a circle around each difference.

Flowers

Flowers grow on many plants. Find out below how they make seeds, then colour the picture.

1. Flowers start as buds with petals packed inside.

2. The buds open up and turn into flowers.

3. Inside each flower is a sweet liquid called nectar.

4. As bees drink the nectar, pollen powder sticks to them.

5. Bees carry pollen to other flowers. The pollen helps plants make seeds.

Seeds are spread by the wind, birds or animals. ----

These flowers grow in different places in the wild.
Press the stickers from the sticker pages onto the grasses.

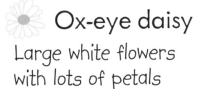 **Ox-eye daisy**

Large white flowers
with lots of petals

 **Bindweed**

Pink or white trumpet-
shaped flowers

 **Wild rose**

Pale pink flowers with
five curved petals

Violet

Purple flowers with
five petals

Cornflower

Blue flowers with lots
of pointed petals

Buttercup

Bright yellow flowers
with rounded petals

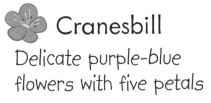 **Cranesbill**

Delicate purple-blue
flowers with five petals

Don't pick
wild flowers.
You might kill the
whole plant.

15

Frogs and toads

Have you ever seen round blobs of jelly in a pond? They're frog eggs, called frogspawn. A mother frog lays them. Number the steps from 1 to 4, to show what happens next.

The tails shrink and disappear. The tadpoles are tiny frogs.

Tiny baby frogs called tadpoles start to grow in the eggs.

They start to grow legs, and their tails start to shrink.

The tadpoles nibble their way out and swim around.

How many tadpoles are there growing in these eggs?

Frogspawn is in big clumps, but toads lay long strings of eggs. Doodle black dots for eggs in the frogspawn and toadspawn.

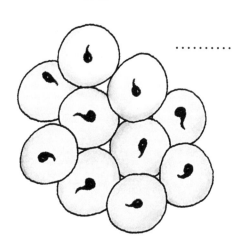

....

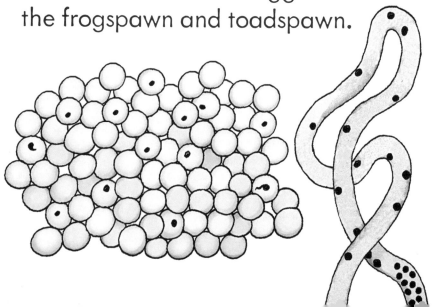

Poppy and Tommy are quietly watching a pond.
How many of each kind of creature can they see?

toad .... frog .... dragonfly ....

This frog is about to hop across the lilypads. It needs to hop on the ones that add up to 10 – which route should it take?

....

....

....

....

....

Spotting puzzles

It's a busy day at the coast. People have come to walk, explore, look at wildlife and watch the waves breaking on the shore. Can you spot all of these little pictures in the big picture?

Lots of people are visiting the countryside and enjoying nature.
Can you spot eight differences between the two pictures?

Weather

Press the stickers from the sticker pages onto this map to show what the weather is like in each place.

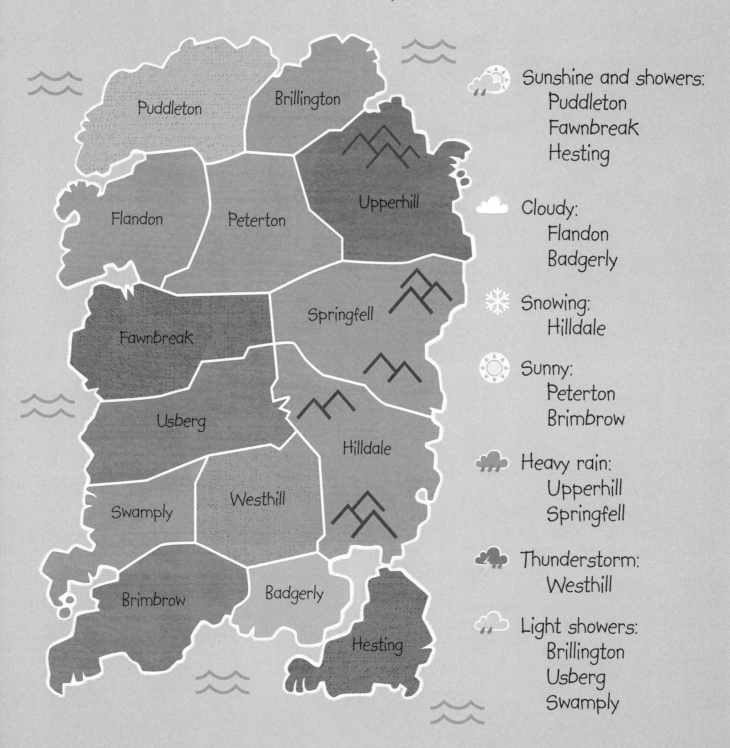

Sunshine and showers:
Puddleton
Fawnbreak
Hesting

Cloudy:
Flandon
Badgerly

Snowing:
Hilldale

Sunny:
Peterton
Brimbrow

Heavy rain:
Upperhill
Springfell

Thunderstorm:
Westhill

Light showers:
Brillington
Usberg
Swamply

Tilly's going for a walk on a hot sunny day. Which four things should she take? Draw around each one.

It's a cold wet day and Billy's going for a muddy walk. Draw around four things he should take with him.

Bright bugs

Colour each of these butterflies so that both sides of their wings match.

Which two butterflies are exactly the same?

Draw a line to take each bee from the flower it's on to a matching flower.

Draw legs and patterns on these
shapes to turn them into bugs.

Spotting birds

An estuary is where a river meets the sea. Fresh river water and salty sea water mix together.

As the tide goes out, birds look for food in the sand and mud. Which square can't you find in the picture – A, B, C or D?

....

A

B

C

D

Can you identify the birds below? Read the descriptions, then link each bird name to the correct picture with a line.

Lapwing – long feathers on head and a greenish back

Oystercatcher – black and white bird with an orange beak

Cormorant – large black bird with big wings and tail

Curlew – dappled brown feathers and a curved beak

Can you spot four differences between these two pictures?

Draw a heron:

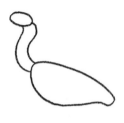 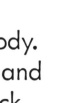 

1. Draw a body. Add a head and a curving neck.

2. Draw a beak and an eye. Add a wing, legs and feet.

3. Colour the heron. Add long feathers on its head.

Draw more herons.

Keeping records

You may want to keep a record of what you see when you're outside. You could write notes, draw pictures or take photos.

Which picture shows all the animals on the list below?

A

B

3 sheep
1 brown horse
1 bumblebee
2 spotty cows
2 rabbits

Picture ....

C

Isla is taking photos on a beach. Looking at the main picture, which photo couldn't she have taken – A, B or C? ....

A

B

C

Stanley's keeping a diary of the birds that he spots. On which day did he see the most birds?

Monday
It was a sunny day and I went for a walk. I saw 3 ducks and 4 geese.

.... birds

Tuesday
It was cold and rainy today, but I did *see* 5 geese. They were looking for food.

.... birds

Wednesday
Another sunny day. I saw 2 ducks and 5 geese, then I saw another duck.

.... birds

Stanley saw most birds on ....

Wildlife garden

People can help wildlife in lots of ways. Below are four things wild creatures like, but the pictures are missing.
Add the stickers from the sticker pages.

A birdbath of water attracts thirsty birds.

Butterflies feed on these tiny flowers.

Beetles like to live among rotting wood.

Flowers such as lavender appeal to bumblebees.

Frogs, snails and other little creatures hide in damp places.
Which snail and frog are hiding in the hole in the ground?

Snail.........and frog..........are hiding in the hole.

This is a bug hotel for bugs and other creatures to live in.
Find the stickers on the sticker pages and put each creature
in the place it will like best.

Ladybirds spend the winter in dry straw.

Old dead wood is a good home for woodlice.

Pieces of old tree bark for centipedes to hide in.

Solitary bees can live in bamboo tubes.

Dry leaves and twigs appeal to beetles.

A dark place for a spider to hide.

Frogs and toads like to be cool and damp.

29

Night...

As night turns to day, some animals go to sleep and others wake up. Can you spot 10 differences between the pictures, apart from any changing colours? Draw around them.

...and day

See if you can find a bird's nest, too.
It's in both pictures.

Lots of beetles

Use bright pens or pencils to colour
these scuttling beetles.

What is nature?
Pages 2-3

Different kinds of animals
Pages 8-9

Flowers   Pages 14-15

Weather   Pages 20-21

Wildlife garden   Pages 28-29

Spider

Bee

Ladybird

Woodlouse

Beetle

Centipede

Toad

Frog

At the seashore Pages 38-39

Homes

Patterns in nature

Picture puzzles

Flying birds

Lovely leaves

Fun things to do

Pebble people

Find pebbles for faces and bodies. Use other natural bits and pieces, too. Then, make funny people or faces.

Leaf pictures

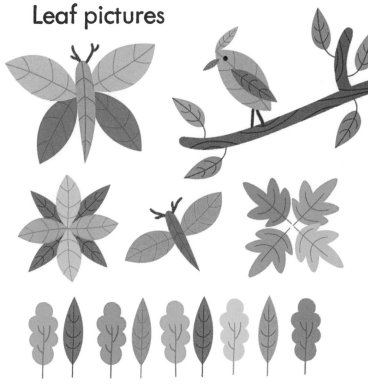

Pick up different leaves that you find on the ground. Use them to make pictures and patterns.

Painted sticks

You could paint patterns or faces, or both, on dry sticks.

Protecting nature

Here are some tips to help you look after nature. There's a sticker of each one on the sticker pages for you to add.

When you're near farm animals, be quiet and calm and move slowly.

Don't pick plants or flowers – they're food for insects and other wildlife.

Follow any rules on signs, such as shutting gates behind you.

Don't touch birds and animals, or their nests and burrows.

If you have a dog, keep it under control, so that it doesn't upset any wildlife.

Never drop litter or leave anything behind when you go home.

Can you help Asha and Jack pick up all the litter?
Draw around 10 pieces of litter as you spot them.

Land, sky and sea

Finish colouring these different landscapes.

Mountain valley

Countryside

Sunset sky

Seashore

At the seashore

Fill this rock pool with creatures and seaweed using the stickers from the sticker pages.

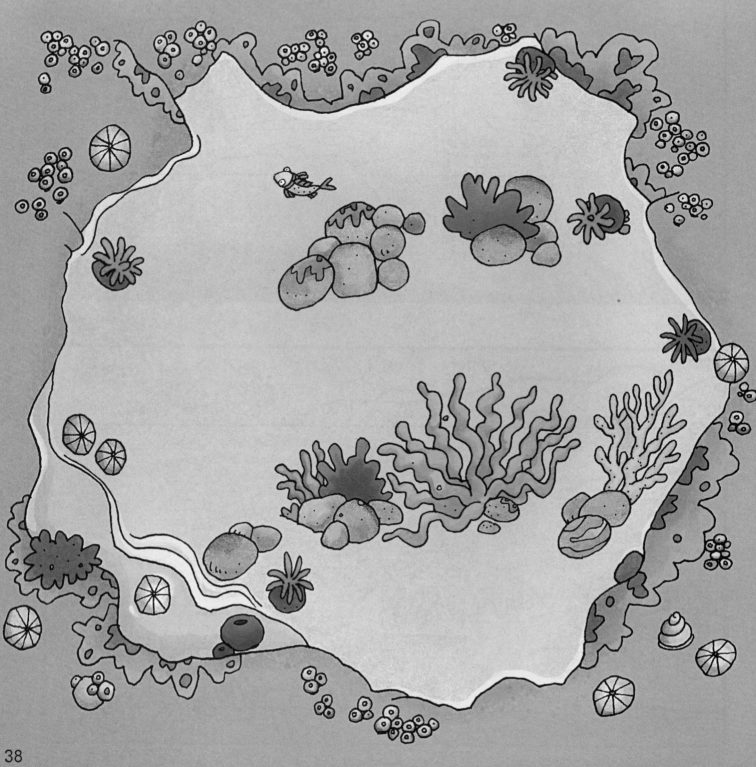

Burrowing worms called lugworms have left these sandy squiggles on a beach. Which two are the same?

..........and

....

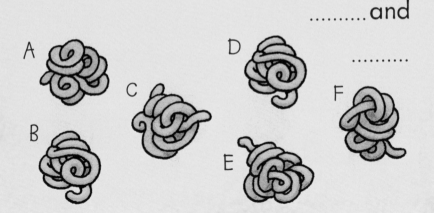

Which piece will complete this broken shell?

....

Draw and colour the other half of this crab.

Join the dots from 1 to 10 to complete this fish.

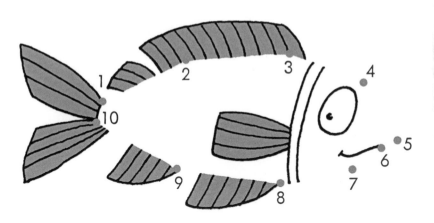

Limpets cling to rocks when the tide goes out. The better they fit, the less they dry out. Which limpet will fit best in the gap?

....

In the woods

Draw on the shapes to make trees and birds.

Here are some ideas...

Tess and Jim are walking in the woods. They've left a trail of sticks and pebbles. Which way should Nancy and Luca go to follow them?

KEY TO SYMBOLS

Turn right

Turn left

Go straight
ahead

Don't go
this way

Shout out
"We're here"

Tess

Jim

Nancy

Luca

Homes

Animals and birds build, dig or find their homes.
Some even carry them around.

These homes need a creature to live in or on them.
Add the creatures using the stickers from the sticker pages.

thrush's nest   spider's web

rabbit's burrow   fox's den   owl's nesting hole

Snails' shells are their homes. Press a sticker shell onto
each snail. Doodle eye stalks on them, too.

Eye stalks

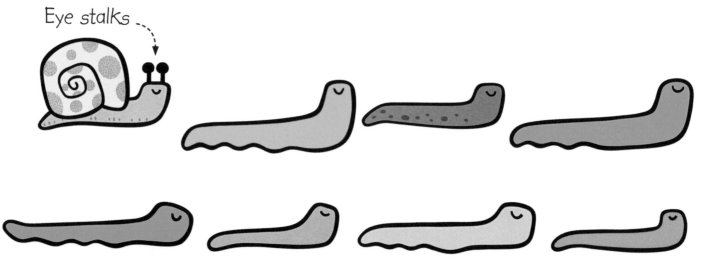

Patterns in nature

The patterned stickers on the sticker pages are close-ups from the pictures below. Press each sticker next to the correct picture.

tiny veins
on a leaf

a spiral
on a shell

stripes in
a rock

spots on
a butterfly

scales
on a fish

little lines
on a feather

Scavenger hunt

Can you spot everything on the list in the picture?
As you find each thing, tick it off the list.

a pine
cone

a magpie's
feather

pebbles

a leaf from
an ash tree

rose petals
that fell to
the ground

sheep's wool that was caught on a fence

a snail shell

a conker (horse chestnut) case

a twig that fell from a tree

half a broken gull's egg

1. A bumpy pine cone
2. Something spiral-shaped
3. A stem with lots of small leaves
4. Something spotty
5. A spiky seed case
6. Smooth pebbles
7. Something fluffy
8. Something black and white
9. Parts of a flower
10. Something made of wood

Picture puzzles

Finish this picture of flowers.

Fill in these three flowers using any colours you like.

Colour the white petals, following the pattern of colours.

Use the petal stickers from the sticker pages to finish this flower.

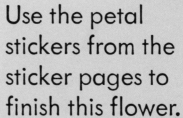

Number these pictures from 1 to 4 to show the order
they should go in.

Can you spot five differences? Draw a circle around each one.

Bird behaviour

Different kinds of birds nest in different places. Look at the picture below. Which kind nests in trees, which nests at the coast, and which nests in the city?

Starling
....

Woodpigeon
....

Kittiwake
....

Each kind of bird has a different song. Great tits sing 'tea-cher tea-cher'. Which bird is singing this song? ....

tea-cher cher-cher

tea-tea tea-cher

cher-tea tea-cher

tea-cher tea-cher

tea-cher tea-tea

A

B

C

D

E

Most birds feed on worms, insects, grubs or seeds. Turn these fingerprints into hungry birds.

Give the birds beaks, eyes, legs, wings and tails.

These birds are having a drink and washing their dusty feathers. Join the dots from 1 to 10 to complete them.

Baby animals

Draw a line between each baby animal and its mother.

deer

badger

fox

fawn

foal

cub

pup

horse

Some animals lay eggs. Babies grow inside the eggs before they hatch. Follow the steps to draw a baby turtle for each egg that's hatched.

1. Draw a shell and a head.

2. Add eyes and a tail.

3. Draw four flippers.

Hungry animals

This fox is hunting for food. Can you spot a mouse hiding from it?

How many rabbits are looking for tasty plants in this vegetable patch?

....

Which way does this mole need to go to catch a worm that's wriggled into one of its tunnels?

Flying birds

When you look up at the sky, watch how birds fly.
They flap their wings, soar up and glide down.

Birds fly in patterns called flight paths. Below are three different kinds – draw over each one.

buzzard

woodpecker

mallard

Some birds of prey hover as they look for food. This kestrel has spotted a mouse, but which one?

....

A   B   C   D

Press on the three stickers from the sticker pages to complete the pattern of flying geese above.

Some birds look very different from each other as they fly. Draw a line between each bird picture and its matching shape.

mallard

heron

gull

magpie

jay

crow

53

Nature in the city

Even in busy cities, there's lots of nature.

Can you spot all of these in the picture?

 five pigeons

 two mallard ducks

 six sparrows

 ivy growing on a building

 three gulls

 five dandelion plants

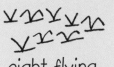 eight flying geese

 four rats

 three squirrels

 one butterfly

Spiders

Most spiders make webs to catch food. These pictures show a spider making a web. Put them in order from 1 to 3.

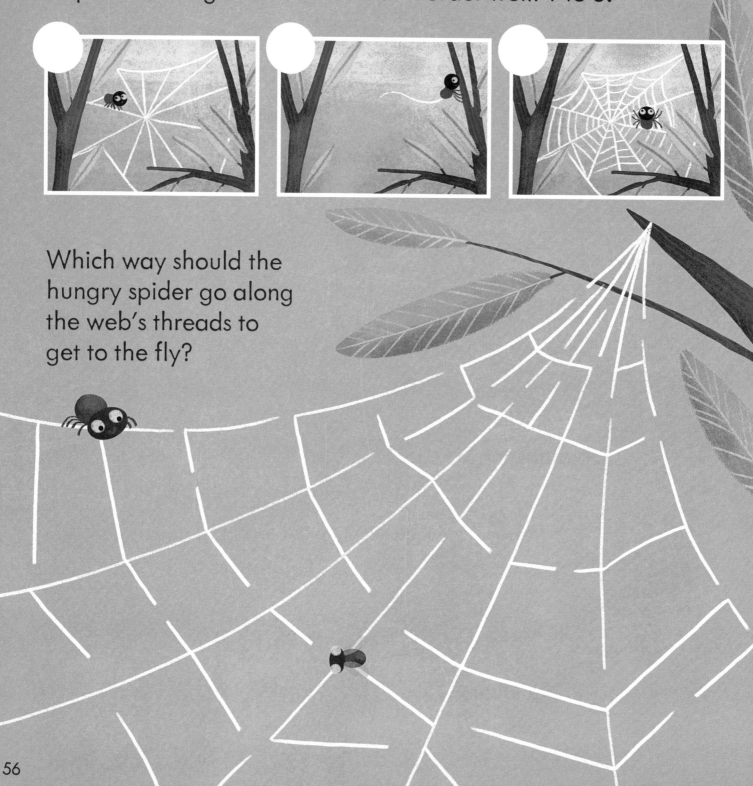

Which way should the hungry spider go along the web's threads to get to the fly?

Spiders live in lots of different places. There are two spiders in each of the pictures below. Can you spot them?

Draw a spider:

1. Draw a head. Add a body above it.

2. Draw eight legs, four on each side.

3. Add eyes and a mouth, then colour the spider.

Add a spider to each web.

Lovely leaves

Most plants, including trees, have leaves. Leaves come in many different shapes and sizes. Draw over the lines below to find out which tree each leaf is from.

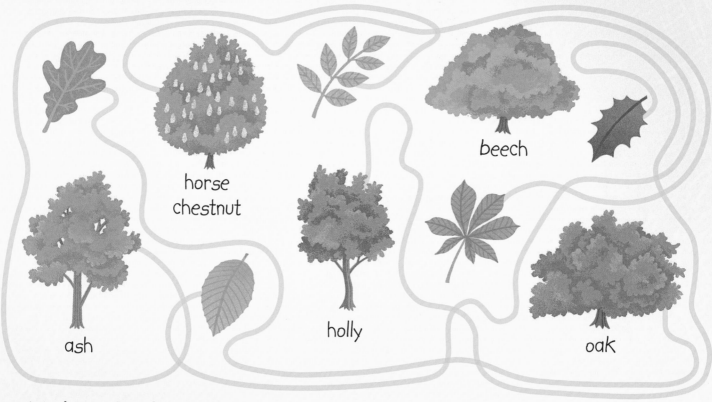

beech

horse chestnut

ash

holly

oak

Make a leaf rubbing:

1. Find a leaf on the ground. Lay it on a piece of paper with its back facing up.

2. Lay a thin piece of paper over the leaf. Rub over it with the side of a crayon.

3. A leaf shape will appear on the paper.

Make each leaf below into a bird, animal or monster. Press on eye stickers from the sticker pages, then draw on the leaves.

Nature at night

As night falls, some animals go to sleep.
Others wake up and hunt for food.
They are called nocturnal animals.

Which bat is flying in front
of the Moon – A, B, C or D?

A

B

C

D

Fireflies' tummies flash
with light. Colour these
tummies yellow.

Which of these moths doesn't
have a matching partner?

1

2

3

4

5

6

7

Answers

2-3 What is nature?

7 ducks are flying by.

4-5 Signs and clues

B Fox   A Badger
C Deer   D Rat

The duck left C. The other prints are:
A – sparrow, B – pigeon, D – heron.

Mouse C made the nest.

6-7 Plants and trees

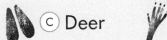

Seedling F is tallest.
There are six matching pairs:

10-11 Insects

The spider is not an
insect. It has eight legs.

D   C   A   B

12-13 Bird life

A – 6 eggs, B – 7 eggs, C – 4 eggs.
Nest B has most eggs in it.
Female – route B, male – route 2.

16-17 Frogs and toads

10 tadpoles are growing in the eggs.

 ◯ 5   ◯ 4   ◯ 6

A – 8, B – 10,
C – 9.
The frog
should take
route B.

18-19 Spotting puzzles

20-21 Weather

22-23 Bright bugs

24-25 Spotting birds

A
B
C
D

Square C isn't in the picture.

Cormorant   Curlew

Lapwing---   Oystercatcher---

26-27 Keeping records

All the animals are in picture C.

◯ sheep   ◯ spotty cows
◯ brown horse   ◯ rabbits
◯ bumblebee

Isla couldn't have taken photo B.

Monday – 7 birds, Tuesday – 5 birds, Wednesday – 8 birds. Stanley saw most birds on Wednesday.

28-29 Wildlife garden

Snail A and frog D are in the hole.

30-31 Night... ...and day

⭕ differences   ⭕ nest

34-35 Protecting nature

38-39 At the seashore

Squiggles B and D are the same.
Piece C will complete the shell.
Limpet B will fit best in the gap.

40-41 In the woods

44-45 Scavenger hunt

⭕ 1. pine cone   ⭕ 6. pebbles
⭕ 2. snail shell   ⭕ 7. sheep's wool
⭕ 3. ash leaf   ⭕ 8. feather
⭕ 4. gull's egg   ⭕ 9. rose petals
⭕ 5. conker case   ⭕ 10. twig

46-47 Picture puzzles

48-49 Bird behaviour

Starling – city, Woodpigeon – trees,
Kittiwake – coast.

Bird D is singing the song.

50 Baby animals

51 Hungry animals

There are 5 rabbits.

52-53 Flying birds

The kestrel has spotted mouse B.

54-55 Nature in the city

○ pigeons
○ ducks
○ sparrows
○ ivy
○ gulls

○ dandelions
○ geese
○ rats
○ squirrels
○ butterfly

56-57 Spiders

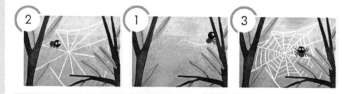

60 Nature at night

Bat A is flying in front of the Moon.

Moth 4 doesn't have a matching partner.

Additional design by Holly Lamont and Katie Webb

Photos page 59 © Thinkstock.